D0281868

If You're Glad I'll be Frank

NIGEL & DIANE PARMENTER
CROXLEY WOOD HOUSE
CROXLEY HALL WOOD
RICKMANSWORTH
HERTS WD3 3BE
Telephone: (0923) 773688
Ansaphone: (0923) 777227

No: *C18 STO · 6*

by the same author

ROSENCRANTZ AND GUILDENSTERN ARE DEAD

THE REAL INSPECTOR HOUND

ENTER A FREE MAN

ALBERT'S BRIDGE

AFTER MAGRITTE

JUMPERS

ARTIST DESCENDING A STAIRCASE and

WHERE ARE THEY NOW

TRAVESTIES

DIRTY LINEN

LORD MALQUIST AND MR. MOON
(novel)

If You're Glad I'll be Frank

A Play for Radio
by
TOM STOPPARD

FABER & FABER
3 Queen Square London

First published in 1969
as 'Albert's Bridge' and 'If You're Glad I'll be Frank'
by Faber and Faber Limited
3 Queen Square, London WC1
First published in this new edition 1976
Printed in Great Britain by
Whitstable Litho, Whitstable
All rights reserved

ISBN 0 571 11102 5

All rights whatsoever in this play are strictly reserved and professional applications for permission to perform it, etc., must be made in advance, before rehearsals begin, to Fraser and Dunlop (Scripts) Ltd., of 91 Regent Street, London W.1., and amateur applications for permission to perform it, etc. must be made in advance, before rehearsals begin, to Samuel French Ltd., of 26 Southampton Street, London W.C.2

CONDITIONS OF SALE
This book is sold subject to the condition that it shall not, by way of trade or otherwise, be lent, re-sold, hired out or otherwise circulated without the publisher's prior consent in any form of binding or cover other than that in which it is published and without a similar condition including this condition being imposed on the subsequent purchaser

© *1969 by Tom Stoppard*

If You're Glad I'll be Frank received its first production on the BBC Third Programme on 8th February 1966.
The cast was as follows:

FRANK	Timothy West
GLADYS	Patsy Rowlands
1ST PORTER	Brian Hewlett
MYRTLE TRELAWNEY	Isabel Rennie
MR. MORTIMER	Henry Stamper
MR. COURTENAY-SMITH	Noel Howlett
SIR JOHN	Alan Haines
LORD COOT	Austin Trevor
BERYL BLIGH	Eva Haddon
OPERATOR	Elizabeth Proud
IVY, *a bus conductoress*	Barbara Mitchell
2ND PORTER	Henry Stamper

Produced by John Tydeman

From her first words it is apparent that GLADYS *is the "TIM" girl, and always has been.*

As such, she has two columns to herself.

The right-hand column is for the Speaking Clock, and as such it is ostensibly continuous. But of course we hear her voice direct, not through a telephone unless otherwise indicated.

The left-hand column is for her unspoken thoughts, and of course this one has the dominant value.

It should be obvious in the script when her "Tim" voice is needed in the background as counterpoint, and when it should be drowned altogether by the rising dominance of her thoughts.

When her "TIM" voice intrudes again I have indicated this not *by the actual words she uses, because the actual time she announces should be related to the number of minutes or seconds that have passed (i.e. depending on the pace of the broadcast) but by suggesting the* space of time *that her speaking voice should take up, and this appears in the script in this form: (3–4 seconds).*

GLADYS *operates the pips too, and these are indicated thus: (*PIP PIP PIP*).*

Some of GLADYS's *sustained passages fall into something halfway between prose and verse, and I have gone some way to indicate the rhythms by line-endings, but of course the effect should not be declamatory.*

Scene 1

FRANK, *who turns out to be a bus driver, is heard dialling "TIM".*

> GLADYS (*through phone*): At the third stroke it will be eight fifty-nine precisely.

FRANK (*amazed disbelief*): It can't be. . . .

(PIP PIP PIP.)

. . . At the third stroke it will be eight fifty-nine and ten seconds. . . .

(*Fearful hope*): It's not. . . ?

(PIP PIP PIP.)

. . . At the third stroke it will be eight fifty-nine and twenty seconds. . . .

(*Joy.*) It is! . . . *Gladys!* It's my Gladys! (*Fade.*)

(PIP PIP PIP.)

Scene 2

Exterior mid traffic, Big Ben begins its nine a.m. routine. Cut to interior: no traffic, Big Ben fainter.

PORTER (*murmurs*): Nine o'clock. Here we go.
  (*What happens is this:* MYRTLE, MORTIMER, COURTENAY-SMITH, SIR JOHN *and the* FIRST LORD OF THE POST OFFICE (LORD COOT) *enter from the street on the first, third, fifth, seventh and ninth strokes of Big Ben respectively (the second, fourth, sixth and eighth strokes being heard through the closed door.) Each opening of the door lets in traffic sound momentarily and amplifies Big Ben.*)
  (*Street door.*)
PORTER: Morning, Mrs. Trelawney.
MYRTLE (*gay*): Hello, Tommy.
  (*And out through door.*)
  (*Street door.*)
PORTER: Morning, Mr. Mortimer.
MORTIMER (*tired*): Good morning, Tom.
  (*And out through door.*)
  (*Street door.*)

8

PORTER: Good morning, Mr. Courtenay-Smith.

C.-SMITH (*vague*): Morning, Mr. Thompson.

(*And out through door.*)

(*Street door.*)

PORTER: Good morning, Sir John.

SIR JOHN (*aloof*): Ah, Thompson. . . .

(*And out through door.*)

(*Street door.*)

PORTER: Good morning, my Lord.

1ST LORD: Morning, Tommy. (*Conspiratorial.*) Anything to report?

PORTER: All on schedule, my Lord.

1ST LORD: Jolly good.

(*Through door.*)

MYRTLE: Good morning, your Lordship.

1ST LORD: Good morning, Mrs. Trelawney.

(*Through door.*)

MORTIMER: Good morning, my Lord.

1ST LORD: Good morning, ah, Mortimer.

(*Through door.*)

C.-SMITH: Good morning, Lord Coot.

1ST LORD: Good morning, Mr. Courtenay-Smith.

(*Through door.*)

SIR JOHN: What ho, Cooty.

1ST LORD: Morning, Jack.

(*Through door.*)

BERYL: Good morning, sir.

1ST LORD (*startled*): Who are you?

BERYL: I'm new.

(*Pause.*)

1ST LORD: I thought I couldn't account for you. . . . New what?

BERYL: New secretary, sir . . . Miss Bligh. They sent me over from Directory Enquiries last night.

1ST LORD: I see. What happened to my old—to Miss—er——

BERYL: Apparently she cracked, sir, at 1.53 a.m. I came at once.

1ST LORD: That's the ticket. The Post Office never sleeps. Do you know the form round here?

BERYL: Well. . . .

1ST LORD: Quite simple. I'm the First Lord of the Post Office, of course. I'm responsible for the lot, with special attention to the Telephone Services, which are as follows—write them down——

UMP—dial-the-Test-score.

SUN—dial-the-weather.

POP—dial-a-pop.

BET—dial-the-racing-results.

GOD—dial-the-Bible-reading.

EAT—dial-a-recipe.

And so on, with many others, including the most popular and important of them all—TIM, dial-the-speaking-clock. We can't afford to lose track of time, or we'd be lost.

Now, you see, we must keep a continuous check on all of them, because if you don't keep an eye on them they slide back. The strain is appalling, and the staffing problems monumental.

Shall we start checking, then? To begin with, synchronize our watches, and then check with TIM—ready? I make it just coming up to nine two and forty seconds. . . .

Scene 3

Follows straight on with the Time signal (PIP PIP PIP).
Heard direct, i.e. not through phone, as is GLADYS now.

GLADYS:

. . . At the third stroke it will be nine two and fifty seconds. . . .

(PIP PIP PIP.)

. . . At the third stroke it will be nine three precisely.

Or to put it another way, three minutes past nine, precisely, though which

(PIP PIP PIP.)

nine in particular, I don't
say, so what's precise
about that? . . .

. . . nine three and ten
seconds. . . .
(PIP PIP PIP.)

The point is beginning to be
    lost on me.
Or rather it is becoming a
    different point.
Or rather I am beginning
    to see through it.
Because they think that
    time is something they
    invented,
for their own convenience,
and divided up into ticks
    and tocks
and sixties and twelves
and twenty-fours . . .
so that they'd know when
    the Olympic record has
    been broken
and when to stop serving
    dinner in second-class
    hotels,
when the season opens and
    the betting closes,
when to retire;
when to leave the station,
renew their applications
when their subscriptions
    have expired;
when time has run out.
So that they'd know how
    long they lasted,
and pretend that it matters,
and how long they've got,

11

as if it mattered,
so that they'd know that we
    know that they know.
That we know, that is.
That they know, of course.

And so on.

                        (Faint time clock, 2–3
                        seconds.)

Ad infinitum.

I used to say ad nauseum
but it goes on long after you
    feel sick.
And I feel sick.
When you look down from
    a great height
you become dizzy. Such
    depth, such distance,
such disappearing tininess so
    far away,
rushing away,
reducing the life-size to
    nothing—
it upsets the scale you live by.
Your eyes go first, followed
    by the head,
and if you can't look away
    you feel sick.
And that's my view of time;
and I can't look away.
Dizziness spirals up between
    my stomach and my head
corkscrewing out the stopper
But I'm empty anyway.
I was emptied long ago.

Because it goes on,

this endless dividing up into
   equal parts,
this keeping track—
because time viewed from
   such distance
etcetera
rushing away
reducing the lifespan to
   nothing
and so on—
(*Pause.*)
The spirit goes first, followed
   by the mind.
And if you can't look away
   you go mad.

                                  (*Time clock, 2–3 seconds.*)

Scene 4

FRANK *dialling; excited, intense. Ringing tone breaks off.*
OPERATOR *is heard through phone.*

OPERATOR: Number please.

FRANK: Listen, do all you people work in the same building?

OPERATOR: This is the operator—can I help you?

FRANK: I want to speak to Gladys Jenkins.

OPERATOR: What's the number, please?

FRANK: She works there—she's in the telephones, you see.

OPERATOR: Hello, sir—operator here——

FRANK: I want to be transferred to Mrs. Jenkins—this is her
   husband.

OPERATOR: Mrs. Jenkins?

FRANK: Speaking clock.

OPERATOR: Do you want to know the time?

FRANK: No—I want my Gladys! What's her number?

OPERATOR: Speaking clock?

FRANK: Yes.

OPERATOR: TIM.

FRANK: Her *number*.

OPERATOR: T-I-M.

FRANK: I demand to speak to your superior——

OPERATOR: Just a moment, sir, putting you through.

GLADYS (*through phone*): . . . At the third stroke it will be nine twelve and forty seconds. . . .

FRANK: It's all right, Glad—it's me again—Frank!

(GLADYS's *timespeak continues underneath.*)

Can you hear me now, Glad?—I've had a time of it I can tell you—I must say, you gave me a turn! So that's where you got to—Gladys? Give over a minute, love—it's Frank—— Can you hear me, Gladys? Give me a sign?

(*Pause; timeclock.*)

I know your voice—it's you, isn't it Gladys—are they holding you?—I'll get you out of there, Gladys—I'll speak to the top man—I'll get the wheels turning, Gladys! I'll pull the strings, don't you worry, love—— But I've got to dash now, love—I'm calling from the terminus and we're due out——

(IVY, *a bus conductress breaks in.*)

IVY: Frank *Jenkins!* The passengers are looking at their watches!

FRANK (*to* IVY): Just coming. (*To* GLADYS.) That was Ivy, my conductress—you don't know Ivy—I'm on a new route now, the 52 to Acton—— Keep your chin up, Glad—you can hear me can't you? I'll be giving you another ring later—— Good-bye, Gladys—oh, Gladys—what's the time now?

GLADYS: Nine fourteen precisely——

FRANK: Thanks, Glad—oh, *thank* you, Gladys! (*He rings off.*)

IVY (*off*): Frank—it's nine fourteen—remember the schedule!

FRANK (*going*): Hey, Ivy—I've found her—I've found my Gladys!

Scene 5

GLADYS (*direct voice now*):

> . . . At the third stroke
> it will be nine fourteen
> and twenty seconds. . . .
> (PIP PIP PIP.)

. . . At the third stroke . . .
I don't think I'll bother, I
don't think there's any point.
Let sleeping dogs and so on.
Because I wouldn't shake it off
by going back, I'd only be in
the middle of it,
with an inkling of infinity,
the only one who has seen both
   ends
rushing away from the middle.
You can't keep your balance
   after that.
Because they don't know what
   time is.
They haven't experienced the
   silence
in which it passes
impartial disinterested
godlike.
Because they didn't invent it at all.
They only invented the clock.
And it doesn't go tick
and it doesn't go tock
and it doesn't go pip.
It doesn't go anything.
And it doesn't go anything for
   ever.
It just goes,
before them, after them, without
them,

15

above all without them,
and their dialling fingers,
their routine-checking, schedule-
    setting time-keeping clockwork—
luminous, anti-magnetic,
fifteen-jewelled self-winding,
grandfather, cuckoo, electric
shock-, dust- and waterproofed,
    chiming;
it counts for nothing against the
    scale of time,
and makes them tiny, bound and
    gagged to the minute-hand
as though across a railway line—
struggling without hope, eyes busy
    with silent-screen distress
as the hour approaches—the express
swings round the curve towards
    them
(and the Golden Labrador who
    might have saved them
never turns up on time).

                              (*2–3 seconds.*)

And they count for nothing
    measured against
the moment in which a glacier
    forms and melts.
Which does not stop them from
    trying
to compete;
they synchronize their watches,
count the beats,
to get the most out of the little
    they've got,
clocking in, and out,
and speeding up,
keeping up with their time-tables,
and adjusting their tables to keep

16

up with their speed,
and check one against the other
and congratulate each other—
a minute saved to make another
   minute possible somewhere else
to be spent another time.
Enough to soft-boil a third of an egg:
hard-boil a fifth.

                              Precisely. . . .
                              (PIP PIP PIP.)
                              (*3–4 seconds.*)

Of course, it's a service if you like.
They dial for twenty second's worth
   of time
and hurry off contained within it
until the next correction,
with no sense of its enormity, none,
no sense of their scurrying
   insignificance;
only the authority of my voice,
the voice of the sun itself,
more accurate than Switzerland—
definitive
divine.

                              (*2–3 seconds, very faint.*)

If it made a difference
I could refuse to play,
sabotage the whole illusion
a little every day if it made a
   difference,
as if it would, if I coughed or
   jumped a minute
(they'd correct their watches by my
   falter).
And if I stopped to explain
At the third stroke it will be   At the third stroke it
                                        will be. . . . (*Continues
                                        3–4 seconds.*)

17

too late to catch up, far
far too late, gentlemen. . . .
they'd complain, to the Post Office
And if stopped altogether,
just stopped, gave up the pretence,
it would make no difference.
Silence is the sound of time passing.

(1–2 seconds, faint.)

Don't ask when the pendulum
   began to swing.
Because there is no pendulum.
It's only the clock that goes tick
   tock
and never the time that chimes.
It's never the time that stops.

(1–2 seconds, quick fade.)

Scene 6

VOICE THROUGH PHONE: . . . thirty minutes in a Regulo 5 oven
   until it is a honey coloured brown. . . . Serves six.
1ST LORD *(ringing off)*: Well, that's that one. Next.
BERYL: That was the last one, sir.
1ST LORD: Then start again at the beginning—continuous
   attention, you see. You'll have to take over this afternoon
   —I have a board meeting.
BERYL: Very good, sir.
1ST LORD: You don't have to call me sir. Call me my Lord.
BERYL: Very good, my Lord.
   (Phone rings.)
   Hello?
FRANK *(through phone)*: This is Frank Jenkins.
BERYL: Yes?
FRANK: It's about my wife.
BERYL: Yes?
FRANK: Is she there?

18

BERYL: This is the First Lord's office.

FRANK: I want the top man in speaking clocks.

BERYL: What name please?

FRANK: Jenkins—it's about my wife, Gladys. She's the speaking clock.

BERYL: Hold on, please.

My Lord, it's a Mr. Jenkins—he says his wife is the speaking clock.

1ST LORD: How extraordinary. Tell him we don't know what he's talking about.

Scene 7

GLADYS (*direct*):

. . . At the third stroke it will be eleven thirty precisely. . . .
(PIP PIP PIP.)

Old Frank. . . .
Yes, we met dancing, I liked him
    from the first.
He said, "If you're Glad
I'll be Frank. . . ."
There was time to laugh then
but while I laughed a bumblebee
fluttered its wings a million times.
How can one compete?
His bus passed my window twice a day,
on the route he had then,
every day, with a toot and a wave
    and was gone.
toot toot toot
everything the same
if only you didn't know,
which I didn't
which I do.
He took his timetable seriously,
    Frank.

19

You could set your clock by him.
But not *time*—it flies by
unrepeatable
and the moment after next the
    passengers are dead
and the bus scrap and the scrap dust,
caught by the wind, blown into the
    crevasse
as the earth splits and scatters
at the speed of bees wings.
Old Frank. He had all the time
in the world for me,
such as it was.

(PIP PIP PIP.)

Scene 8

In the street FRANK's *bus comes to a rather abrupt halt, the door of his cab opens, slams shut as he runs across the pavement and through a door. He is breathless and in a frantic hurry.*

FRANK: Hey, you—who's in charge here?
PORTER: I am. Is that your bus?
FRANK: Who's the top man—quick!
PORTER: You can't park there after seven if the month's got an R in it or before nine if it hasn't except on Christmas and the Chairman's birthday should it fall in Lent.
FRANK: I have an appointment with the chairman.
PORTER (*to the sound of horns*): Seems to be a bit of a traffic jam out there.
FRANK: What floor's he on?
PORTER: He's not on the floor this early. Is this your conductress?
   (*As the door flies open.*)
IVY: Frank—what are you doing!
FRANK: All right, all right! (*To* PORTER.) Listen—I'll be passing your door again at one-fourteen. Tell him to be ready——

20

CONDUCTRESS: Frank—we'll get behind time!
FRANK (*Leaving hurriedly*): It's all right, I got ninety seconds
    ahead going round the park. . . .
    (*And out; and break.*)

Scene 9

In the street FRANK'S *bus draws up once more; same slam, same
feet, same door, same frenzy.*

FRANK: Where is he? I've got ninety-five seconds.
2ND PORTER: Who?
FRANK: Who are you?
2ND PORTER: What do you want?
FRANK: Where's the other porter?
2ND PORTER: Gone to lunch—it's one-fourteen.
FRANK: Never mind him—where's the chairman?
2ND PORTER: They eat together.
    (*Door crashes open.*)
CONDUCTRESS: Frank *Jenkins!*
2ND PORTER: Like brothers.
CONDUCTRESS: What about the schedule!?
FRANK (*to* PORTER): Listen—I'll be back here at two forty-
    seven——
CONDUCTRESS (*almost in tears*): I ask you to remember the
    schedule!
2ND PORTER (*as the horns sound*): Hello—is that your bus out
    there?
FRANK (*leaving hurriedly*): Two forty-seven!—tell him it's about
    Gladys Jenkins!

Scene 10

GLADYS (*through phone*): . . . three fourteen and twenty
    seconds. . . .
    (PIP PIP PIP.)

1ST LORD (*ringing off*): Precisely! Next!

BERYL: God, my Lord.

GOD (*through phone*): In the beginning was the Heaven and the Earth. . . .

    (*Fade.*)

Scene 11

GLADYS (*direct*):

    . . . At the third stroke it will be three fourteen and fifty seconds. . . .

Check, check, check. . . .
One day I'll give him something
to check up for . . .
tick tock
tick tock
check check
chick chock
tick
you can check
your click clock
by my pip pip pip   (PIP PIP PIP.)
I never waver,
I'm reliable,
lord, lord,
I'm your servant,
trained,
precisely.   . . . precisely.

(*With a click* FRANK *is on the line.*)

(*We hear him, as* GLADYS *does, through the phone.*)

FRANK: Hello, Gladys—it's Frank. I bet you wondered where I'd got to. . . . Well, I've had a bit of trouble getting hold of the right man, you see, but don't you worry because the next trip will give me the time—I'll be bang outside his door slap in the middle of the rush hour so I'll have a good four minutes—can you hear me, Gladys? . . .

    (*Breaks a little.*)

22

Oh, Gladys—talk to me—I want you back, I'll let you do
anything you like if you come back—I'll let you be a nun,
if that's what you really want . . . Gladys? I love you,
Gladys——

Hold on, love, hold on a bit, and I'll have you out of
there. . . .

Got to go now, Gladys, Ivy's calling me, we're due out.
Bye bye . . . bye bye. . . . (*Rings off.*)

GLADYS:

I can hear them all
though they do not know enough to
speak to me.
I can hear them breathe,
pause, listen,
sometimes the frogsong of clockwindings
and the muttered repetition to the
nearest minute . . .
but never a question of a question,
never spoken,
it remains open, permanent,
demanding a different answer
every ten seconds.

Until Frank.
Oh, Frank, you knew my voice,
but how can I reply?
I'd bring the whole thing down with a cough,
stun them with a sigh. . . .
(*Sobbing a little.*)
I was going to be a nun, but they wouldn't have me
because I didn't believe, I didn't believe *enough*, that is;
most of it I believed all right, or was willing to believe,
but not enough for their purposes, not about him being
the son of God, for instance, that's the part that put paid
to my ambition, that's where we didn't see eye to eye.
No, that's one of the main points, she said, without that
you might as well believe in a pair of old socks for all the
good you are to us, or words to that effect. I asked her to

23

stretch a point but she wasn't having any of it. I asked her
to let me stay inside without being a proper nun, it made
no difference to me, it was the serenity I was after, that and
the clean linen, but she wasn't having any of that.
(*Almost a wail.*)
But it's not the same thing at all!
I thought it would be—peace!
Oh, Frank—tell them—
I shan't go on, I'll let go
and sneeze the fear of God into
their alarm-setting, egg-timing,
train-catching, coffee-breaking
  faith in
an uncomprehended clockwork—

yes, if I let go,
lost track
changed the beat, went off the rails—
cracked——

	. . . At the third stroke it will be three eighteen and ten seconds. . . .
	(PIP PIP PIP.)
At the third stroke it will be three eighteen and twenty seconds. . . . And so what?	At the third stroke it will be three eighteen and twenty seconds. . . . (PIP PIP PIP.)
At the third stroke it will be too late to do any good, gentlemen——	At the third stroke it will be three eighteen and thirty seconds. . . . (PIP PIP PIP.) At the third stroke. . . .
At the third stroke Manchester City 2, Whores of Lancashire 43 for seven declared	

24

At the third stroke
Sheffield Wednesday will be cloudy
and so will Finisterre. . . .
(*The Queen.*) So a Merry Christmas
and God Bless you everywhere. . . .
And now the Prime Minister!:
Gentlemen, the jig is up—I have
given you tears. . . .
And now the First Lord!—
Don't lose your heads while all
about you on the burning deck. . . .
Oh—Frank! Help me! . . .

Scene 12

FRANK'*s bus stops abruptly. Same place, same slam, same feet,
same door, same frenzy.*

FRANK : Right, let's not waste time—where is she?
PORTER : State your business.
FRANK : I'm looking for my wife.
PORTER : Name?
FRANK : Jenkins—you know me.
PORTER : *Her* name!
FRANK : Sorry—Jenkins.
PORTER : Better. Your name?
FRANK : Jenkins.
PORTER : Relative?
FRANK : Husband.
PORTER : Holds water so far.
FRANK : I demand to see your superior.
PORTER : Name?
FRANK : Jenkins!
PORTER : No one of that name here.
FRANK : I see your game—a conspiracy, is it?
PORTER (*as the horns sound*): Is that your bus out there?

25

FRANK: I demand to speak to the chief of speaking clocks.

PORTER (*as the door bursts open*): Here she comes.

IVY (*conductress*): I'm not covering up for you again, Frank Jenkins!

PORTER: Hey—you can't go in there!

(*Door.*)

MYRTLE: Hello.

FRANK: Where's the top man?

MYRTLE: Keep on as you're going.

(*Door.*)

MORTIMER: Who are you?

FRANK: I want my wife!

MORTIMER: Now, look here, old man, there's a time and place for everything——

FRANK: I want her back!

MORTIMER: My dear fellow, please don't make a scene in the office——

FRANK: You're holding her against her will——

MORTIMER: I think that's for her to say. The fact is Myrtle and I are in love——

FRANK: I want my Gladys.

MORTIMER: Gladys? Isn't your name Trelawney?

FRANK: Jenkins—where's my Gladys?

MORTIMER: Gladys?

FRANK: My wife——

MORTIMER: Are you suggesting that a man of my scrupulous morality——

(*Door.*)

MYRTLE: Darling, there's a bus conductress outside——

MORTIMER: Thank you, Mrs. Trelawney——

IVY (*desperate*): Frank!—the traffic is beginning to move!

FRANK: I demand to see your superior!

MORTIMER: You can't go in there!

(*Door.*)

C.-SMITH: Yes?

FRANK: Are you the top man?

MORTIMER: Excuse me, Mr. Courtenay-Smith, this man just burst into——

26

IVY: Frank—I ask you to think of your schedule!
FRANK: Shut up! You there, are you the top man?
C.-SMITH: In my field, or do you speak hierarchically?
FRANK: I speak of Gladys Jenkins.
C.-SMITH: Not my field——
FRANK: You've got my wife——
MORTIMER: How dare you suggest that a man of Mr.
 Courtenay-Smith's scrupulous morality——
IVY: Frank! the passengers have noticed!
 (*Door.*)
C.-SMITH: Where's he gone?
MYRTLE: Darling, what's going on?
MORTIMER: Mrs. Trelawney, I must ask you to address me——
C.-SMITH: My God—the time-and-motion system won't take
 the strain!
IVY (*fading*): Fra-a-a-nk. . . !

Scene 13

GLADYS (*breaking down slowly but surely*):

At the third stroke
I'm going to give it up,
yes, yes . . . it's asking too much,
for one person to be in the know
of so much, for so many . . .
and at the third stroke
Frank will come
. . . Frank. . . .
I'm going to drop it now,
it can go on without me,
and it will,
time doesn't need me—
they think I'm time, but I'm
not—
I'm Gladys Jenkins and at the
 third stroke

At the third stroke it
will be four twenty-
three and ten
seconds. . . .

27

I'm going to cough,
sneeze
whisper an obscenity that will leave
ten thousand coronaries sprawled
across their telephone tables,
and the trains will run half empty
and all the bloody eggs will turn to
volcanic rock smoking in dry
   cracked saucepans
as soon as I shout—
Ship!
(a vessel)
*Pis*cine!
(pertaining to fishes)
*Fruc!*tuate
(fruit-bearing)
(*She giggles hysterically.*)
oh yes I will
and then they'll let me go
they'll have to
because Frank knows I'm here—
come on, please Frank, I love you
and at the third stroke I will
yes I will yes at the third stroke I
   will. . . .

Scene 14

1ST LORD : Well, gentlemen, in bringing this board meeting to a
close, and I'm sure you're all as bored as I am,
(*Chuckle chuckle, hear hear.*)
I think we must congratulate ourselves on the variety and
consistency of the services which we in the telephone office
have maintained for the public in the face of the most
difficult problems. I believe I'm right in saying that if the
last Test Match had not been abandoned because of the

rain, UMP would barely have lasted the five days, but all
was well as it happened, though the same rainy conditions
did put an extra strain on SUN our weather forecast
service. . . . I don't know if you have anything to add, Sir
John?

SIR JOHN: Well, Cooty—my Lord, that is—only to join with the
rest of the Board in heartily congratulating you on the
excellent report——
(*Hear hear hear hear.*)

1ST LORD: Thank you. Now is there any other business?
(*Door.*)

FRANK (*out of breath*): Where's Gladys Jenkins?!

1ST LORD: There you have me, gentlemen.

SIR JOHN: Point of order, my Lord.

1ST LORD: Yes, Jack?

SIR JOHN: I don't think this man——

FRANK: I'm not taking any more of this—where've you got my
Glad——
(*Door.*)

C.-SMITH: Forgive me, my Lord—this man is quite
unauthorized——

IVY: Frank, the passengers are rioting! All is lost!

MORTIMER: Now look here——

MYRTLE: Darling, do shut up!

FRANK: Damn you. What have you done with my wife?

SIR JOHN: Don't you come here with your nasty little
innuendoes, Trelawney—whatever you may have heard
about the Bournemouth conference, Myrtle and I——

IVY: The passengers are coming!
(FIRST LORD *gets quiet by banging his gavel.*)
(*Pause.*)
(*Noise of rioting passengers.*)

1ST LORD: Gentlemen—please! (*Pause.*) Now what's all the row
about?

IVY: It's the passengers, sir.

FRANK: Are you the top man?

1ST LORD: Certainly.

FRANK: What have you done with my Gladys?

29

MORTIMER: How dare you suggest that a man of the First Lord's scrupulous morality——

1ST LORD: Please, Mr. Mortimer, let him finish.

FRANK: She's the speaking clock.

1ST LORD: What do you mean? *TIM?*

FRANK: Gladys. Yes.

1ST LORD (*chuckling*): My dear fellow—there's no Gladys—we wouldn't trust your wife with the *time*—it's a machine, I thought everyone knew that. . . .

FRANK: A machine?

1ST LORD: He thought it was his wife!

(*General chuckles.*)

Wife . . . thought it was his wife! . . .

FRANK: It was her voice——

IVY: Oh, Frank—they wouldn't use your Glad for that. It's just the speaking clock——

FRANK: She was educated——

IVY: Oh Frank—come on, come on now, we'll be in awful trouble with the Inspector.

FRANK: But Ivy—she *talked* to me. . . .

IVY: She couldn't have done——

1ST LORD: She *talked* to you, my dear fellow?

FRANK: Well, not exactly. . . .

IVY: Of course she didn't. Come on, now. . . .

1ST LORD: That's it—back to your offices gentlemen. We must all make up for lost time.

(*General movement out.*)

FRANK: But she sounded like my Gladys. . . .

IVY: You'll have to go on looking, Frank. . . .

(FIRST LORD *alone.*)

1ST LORD: Dear me, dear me. . . .

(*Door.*)

BERYL (*urgent*): Sir!

1ST LORD: What is it, Miss Bligh?

BERYL: It's the speaking clock—I was just checking it and——

1ST LORD: All right—get me TIM, I'll see to it.

BERYL: Yes, my Lord. (*Dialling.*) She's on now, my Lord.

GLADYS (*through phone. Sobbing hysterically*): At the third stroke it will be five thirty five and fifty seconds. . . .

(PIP PIP PIP.)

1ST LORD: Mrs. Jenkins. . . . This is the First Lord speaking.

GLADYS: At the third stroke it will be five thirty-six
precisely. . . .

1ST LORD: Mrs. Jenkins—pull yourself together, stop crying.
And you've lost forty seconds somewhere by my watch——

GLADYS: At the third stroke I don't know what time it is and I
don't care, because it doesn't go tick tock at all, it just
goes and I have seen—I have seen infinity!

1ST LORD: *Mrs. Jenkins!*

GLADYS (*sniffing*): I can't go on!

1ST LORD: Come on now, this isn't like you at all. Let's get
things back on the rails, hm? Think of the public, Mrs.
Jenkins. . . . Come on now . . . at the third stroke. . . .

GLADYS: At the third stroke. . . .

1ST LORD: It will be five thirty seven and forty seconds.

(PIP PIP PIP.)

Carry on from there. . . .

GLADYS: At the third stroke it will be five thirty-seven and
fifty seconds. . . .

1ST LORD: That's it—spot on Mrs. Jenkins. Control your voice
now.

(PIP PIP PIP.)

GLADYS: At the third stroke it will be five thirty-eight
precisely.

1ST LORD: Well done, Mrs. Jenkins. Well done—I'll check you
again within the hour, as usual. (*Rings off.*)

GLADYS (*direct now*): At the third stroke it
will be five thirty-eight
and ten seconds. . . .

He thinks he's God. . . . (PIP PIP PIP.)

At the third stroke. . . .

(*Fading out.*)